Polarity of Love

Awakening Self-Love

Indi Writes

Poetry

Copyright © 2018: Indira Alves Dias

All rights reserved. No part of this publication may be produced, distributed, or transmitted in any form or by any means, including photocopying, recording, or other electronic or mechanical methods, without the prior written permission of the publisher, except in the case of brief quotations embodied in critical reviews and certain other non-commercial uses permitted by copyright law.

First Printed in United Kingdom 2018

Published by Conscious Dreams Publishing

www.consciousdreamspublishing.com

ISBN: 978-1-912551-44-6

Dedication

Polarity of Love is dedicated to all the lovers in the word. Especially to my maternal and paternal grandparents.

Acknowledgements

Thanks to **Conscious Dreams Publishing** for creating the perfect platform for authors like myself to complete and distribute our work worldwide.

Thanks to **Danni Blechner** who has been like my publishing fairy.

Thank you to my beautiful family, my husband and children who inspire me to be my best and share my work and creativity.

Contents

Part 1 9

- A Fool for Love 13
- Unapologetically ME 15
- Untitled 17
- Ankh with Me 19
- Raw Naturist 21
- Morning Serenade 23
- Journey of a Sailors' Heart 27
- What? 29
- Mr Oppressor 33
- Depths of Love 35
- Angry Goddess 37
- Guilty 41
- Want You Back 43
- Past Broken 47
- Generational Love 49
- Endurance 53
- Self-Lost 55
- Officially Crazy 57
- Raw Lotion on our Ships 61
- Dear Brother 65
- Silent Leader 67
- Polarity of Love 69
- Female Expressions 71

The Birthing 75
A Better Love 77
Eye Am's 79
Her 81

Part 2 .... *83*

Moistured Scriptures 85
Untitled 2 87
God's Love 89
Reptilian 93
Immortal Love 95
Marinated 97
Underneath 99
Jealous God 101
Poker Face 103
Poisoned Antidote 105
Obsession Lover 107
To My Dear Beloved, ... 109
Ugly Truth 113
Love Hack 115
Kiss Her 117
A God After a Woman's Heart 119
Ankhed 121
Goddess Magic 123
Love Me Like the Sun 125

About the Author *127*

Part 1

*The law of polarity tells us that every 1 thing has 2 sides.
Hot is the extreme opposite of Cold,
hot and cold are opposing extremes
of the same one thing which is temperature.
If you have one, you must have the other.
Nothing comes in halves...
Like wise Love and Hate are extreme
opposite poles of the same thing.*

What is love & hate?

Love tides will always entwine us
As old as time...
No one escapes love
The renewal of its healing
To go higher one has to fall first.

Love fallen

A Fool for Love

Come let yourself be loved
Seek your comfort in me
If you choose me, I'll rebuild your world
If you see in me the one you want as your woman
Kiss me as if I am the last woman you'll ever hold
I want to see you shine
Brighter than any star
Just make me your bride, till death do us part
Put your worries on my chest
Till you have it no more.
Find in here the friend to chill, to play, to cry with
Take from me all the love, passion and
excitement you need
Because if I choose you...
You it is
Unless I'm a fool
Then let that be a fool for you...

Unapologetically ME

Like the bible
There's many versions, translations of me
Ya'll keep playing Chinese Whisperers
Thinking I can't hear

I am the wife, the mother
The chick on the side and the other bitch he's looking at

I be cooking that good, good vegan protein
While grinding to Lil Wayne rap
On Blast
Seeking the Spirit all day fasting from
Monday to Sunday
Consecrated, set apart as they say...
Transmuting demons into angels
While dancing with the devil too...
Now you riddle me this
No box can fit over me
I am a Source of infinite universes
Everything even if you fail to see!

I be... poling like a seesaw on polarity
Unapologetically ME

Untitled

You undress me with your mind

To reveal beneath my perfection

Disarm me...

Tease me with your knowledge of all these Universes

Your Soul whispering, lingering, surrounding mine

Each word lands like a leaful arrow onto its target

My heart? Pumps its life

Into your hands...

Smiles...

You haven't even laid a finger on me yet...

Your energy is an element to my magic

Ankh with Me

O, King of my dreams
Love me tonight over this wet pillow
Turn these tears of anguish into sweat of pleasure
Overwhelm our fears, casting daemons diminishing all
laws of Caesar
O, King of my Seals
Love me tonight under this brick ceiling
Break your vows, overstep your boundaries
I am your snake, your Eve
To you Eye hand over the Apple
O, King of my sins
Love me tonight as I lay awake naked
Await the warmth of your tongue
over my breasts
To feel the texture of your caress
Your strong hands delicately choking my neck
O, King of my classroom
Love me tonight as you drink from the river
of knowledge
Yet enslaved to her deserted body
Where the illusion of her Oasis
Is worth the wait of a life time

O, King of my Universe
Love me tonight as you love yourself
With your permission, I'll take you places
I'll do things to you
you may never recall
Yet never forget
Never regret
O, King of consciousness
Love me tonight with your matter and physical
I need to feel your heat, your weight, your
blood pumping
Hold me tight, materialise
The Goddess in me
Make us complete
Masterpiece
Invoke a seed
If you wanna Ankh with me!?

Raw Naturist

When your dick comes into me
Slides in through the fabrics of my vagina
Drowned by the rivers of my emotions
Contracted; abstracted; all these muscles spasms
My body screams to put it in
My body begs to keep it in
You are an element to my pleasure
Your hardworking hands hiking through my skin
Your heart-warming kisses
I can only tell you this:
When you kiss the entrance of all existence factory
When you bow in love and adoration
For this temple, into my temples
Sanctifying, gratifying, satisfying
My pleasurer, the gardener, energiser
You show Adam, I show Eve
King to our Kingdom
Goddess of our Yoniverse
United we uncover the way
Because Us together
We can create all things
In our image and likeness...

Morning Serenade

O, King
The birds brought an orchestra surrounding my home
As if their seasonal journey is now completed
Finally, safely arrived at their destination
They sang so gracefully
Expanding the emotions with each sound
A beautiful symphony with such intensity at the early hours of 5am...
My legs are still weak, my whole body still shaken
From the pleasure you penetrated into me...
I think of you over and over...
holding back, I try to behave but
The purple in your magnetic field breaks down all my walls...
The horns you exposed to my eye
They reap all my fears
And I...
I dance freely
Naked
Covered by my own hair like a gypsy...
For you
My invisible visitor
Lover Reptilian
Master Alchemist
Who breaks down space & distance,
Destroys these chains off my hands
Recreating boundaries, realities, expectations.

All so the gypsy in her heart could dance
For him
Alone
And the light in his eye be sparked
Lit into the heat of her love

The intention to love & the outcome of such love has different appearances especially when we do not know ourselves...
Eye wish You Love, I wish You life.

Journey of a Sailors' Heart

Just as sure dawn will fall
Soon my boat will arrive your coast...
The compass indicates South.
Yet instincts point North.
You're always there. Immovable.
Heart cold, hard as a rock

Obnoxious, disgusting pirates threaten my heart.
Even make me smile sometimes. Haha!!

You don't flinch – you just won't!

How can I then see the sun in your eyes at the sight of me?

The longitude between us, won't keep us apart.
Your black, dark heart won't stop me departing.
I will fight, cry, die...
On each nautical mile... farther away...
You've been my beautiful beast – the cure and the cause
Why push me away, making this Ocean seem false??
Yet I follow the current, keeps bringing me back...

As the salt belongs to the Ocean
The sun is always untouchable
Even at sunrise...

What?

What under these sunny heavens
Possesses a woman
To so eagerly, evilly, consistently
Yearns & strives to deliver
The humiliation of her own soul aches
Upon a sister
Whose only crime was catch her Mister's EYE
Her only fall was to love him back
So, so good, oh yea that's right!
It was so much more than the youth of her smile
Which birthed jealousy
In the wombman whom had birthed his begotten child
A rejection which breed with the other's scent
All over his mouth
Like witchcraft
No craft could break
So, baby step by baby step,
She nurses her own craze
Wrapped up in hate
Over what?
What over these hells!!??
Condemns such Goddesses to destroy
Over no God...
No God
He was No God
Release your wraths
For Gods do not make you cry

Neither do they test your strength
The throne is yours beloved
You're only competing with yourself
Goddess, Goddess
She's not your enemy
Rather your heart which hurts
Ponders, wonders, fond of
Blinded, used, abused by the true enemy
A lover with no love
A brother of whom you were no sister to
Betrayed by the beautiful beast you claimed beloved
What under such emotions
Shall you find?
When you've destroyed earth
Will you realise
Traps, lies whereupon you crave to lay
Whose hands you desperately yearned their touch
Yearning a true God's embrace
Beloved sister walk away.

What is love!!??
When the broken pieces keep piercing through the ligaments which holds you together!??
What is love when she can't even recognise that which is upmost devoted to her highest existence...!??
What is the love of the world
In comparison to the yearns of her Soul...!??
What is love when there's fear... Beloved...?

Mr Oppressor

Mr Oppressor,
Mr Go Fool Yourself!
When will you accept her birth of your soul?
When will you understand her desire is to sit you on
a throne!?
She's a tree of life...
Stop chopping her because you think you can
make paper
– you're trying to kill her!
Stop cutting her down because society told you money is
a necessity...
You may know amounts, you know not value...
You made it so hard to love
That she cannot even love you now...
Demanded every essence of her,
Scraped her skin, ripped her organs
To reach her bones...
Even so, it wasn't enough for you...
Even the air she breathes, you took it...
Left her breathless
The incubator of your offspring...
Yet you claim loving her...
Indulge in her essence,
Rather than take her essence to satisfy you physically!!
She is life altogether
She's God
And if you are chosen

She can be your Godness
However, brother beware
It is self-love you seek in her
She'll guide you there, for she knows
You must earn your own...
Stop destroying her or she'll walk away
From you projecting so much self-hate!

Depths of Love

What is this love of yours?
Takes no pleasure in my smile
Who is this wife of yours?
Who you insist endures so much pain
Your favourite sight
Isn't it her crying?
So, tell me Mister,
Do you not feel her body tense up?
Every time you please yourself in her?
Can you really not see her soul trembling
Her heart pumping begging you to stop
So fearful that she may say it out loud?
A prisoner in her own mind
In custody of your love
Mr Oppressor go ahead and oppress her
Until the day she fights back
Reduce her to nothing then ask
What is wrong with you?
You see Sir, what you don't see
Won't seem to realise, take notice of
The level of her fertile ground is high
It goes beyond her Godness
The force of Karma naturally
Makes you reap what you sow
Now that's cold...
No need to say I told you so

Your ignorant torture cannot break her Soul
Mother Nature only Knows of
Unconditional and tough Love

Angry Goddess

While I made a God out of you
You conspire to steal my powers
You plough to destroy my essence
The heart of love which brought you to an awakening
The same you insist in suffocating
You seek to cease
Turn me deceased
Slice my tongue
Evil words you speak
Be sure that the path to my destruction
Thou shall never reach
I created you creator
Then you create yourself into my enemy
I gave you my key
With hopes it would save you
I loved you with pure love
But you weren't used to it
Now look into me
I adore you still
My love believe me:
I did not come from your rib
Because true Gods come through the womb
Uterus

We're not crazy for yearning desires!
We're in-this-sanity tied in-motion-lies…
Or-Cosmic flowing;
Through physical tides.

Guilty

I plead guilty
Grinning my teeth
Accept all accusations
An extra glass
I missed you so
Loving you has been overfilled,
Spilled
Cannot be contained
Your scent on my skin
So intense beyond control
Giving in to my soul desire
Even if it all seems wrong
It's never felt so right
Hard nipples on my breasts
Smiling and blushing
Our rivers overflowing
It's not what we do
But the depth of who we become
when we connect
in this essence
all mysteries become revealed
Like waking up from
a thousand years of deep sleep...
Being birthed out of a mother's womb
Life can be such an ecstasy
I plead guilty!
Guilty for such life...

Guilty for the moisture in your lips
Guilty for love
For not waiting until the next lifetime!
Bliss
You are where I belong
In this box we still fly away
You the key, Eye the door
My Soul
Now I do know
Soul mate, Soul God
You've been there all along
Love of my life.

Want You Back

You're gonna want me back!!
You're gonna miss me when you're gone...
Said death in her Eye
Thirsty & Lustfully
Yearning for his Heart,
... Mind,
... Life,
Oh His Might...
You'll be back into my palm
Prophesied her – Her Power in Sound!!
Like the very first time,
True unconditional love at its prime
You'll be hunted by my scent,
Tormented in your dreams
Cursed him in her hate!!!
Awakened by unexplained pleasure
Screaming my name...
Fulfilled by my Soul quest
Said the devil in her heart.
Yearning his touch, warmth, just once more...
Like his smoke in her lungs...
His rum in the streams of her blood...
Rushing through the wrongs of love,
Their lives in his intoxicated hands
Teasing whilst he's speeding through the motorway...

Only makes sense to the insane
Crazy enough to embrace
The truths of falling higher
Into the EVILS of LOVE...
I still want you back!!
Awakened, tormented
Hunted by your unfulfilling pleasure
Delivered from the nightmares of your misses
Amidst her most moist intimate wishes
Of wanting you back
Yearning you more
Taking away my breath
As you park in the early hours outside a hotel
Loving you
Whilst you're loving me
Bring back the toxins we called love
I miss you most now that I'm gone...

*A broken heart tears its salt
from time to time...
It is only broken if it lacks
self-love.*

Past Broken

I am way past broken
I be like the dead walking
Only seeing my light when you recognise it
Why am I contained within your gaze?
What's love worth if not reflected?
What am I really if I can't see me eye to eye?
Who can I be if I need you to see me...!!?
And need you... to see me.
So, I get to feel me
Deeper...
Taste the Neters
Sweeter...
O, lover of my Soul
Yearner of this secret love
Love me better
For I am way past broken...

Generational Love

Poetry is my love
Healing essences of my own brokenness
To help my father disgraced me
Almost burned as his disgrace is;
Elevating my lover, all efforts I gave
Drowned me in my own tears...
Lonesome, disrespect, side chicks and fears

...

As I look up in hope
To raise a Sun off the son of my womb
My shaken hands taste the salt
Onto each finger which wiped these tears through ought all these years
What is this flame that keeps me firing forth!?
It's incredible the things I have endured...
Oh son, my sun;
Fruit of my womb
Flesh of my flesh
Bone of my bones
Essence of our Soul
Hope is for fools,
And fools aren't we all!!??
The works of a mother
Broken by each father, each lover
Never refusing to flow and blow
Her inner nature...
Broken, still whole.

Whist some say love is the answer,
Others claim it may just be the cause.
Love is only blind when you have your eye closed.

Endurance

Now I must endure it longer
Hearing you spill the evil things
All the inadequacies I may have committed
Through in and out your abuse
How obscure
Professional narcissism
If the victim is you, why am I the one chasing away?
If indeed you pilgrim to my love
Why don't you respect the humps you stump upon!??
Demanding for love!
Such powerful warrior
Such range unattended
Blinded he slays his lover
As opposed to opponent...
A death guilty for love...
A life lived in its lack
How much longer will I endure...?
How much deeper can you beat me?
How deeply engraved do the spirits require this
lesson sanskared
Upon within?
How much longer must I endure
The world's so-called love?

Self-Lost

How can you be in an abusive relationship and
don't know it?
How did your grandiosity crack?
Silently. So desperately you fight to hold it...
You hold on to the cause
With your bleeding hands
Piercing deeper into your already cuts
But without him...
There's no blood, no cuts no broken pieces and
dispersed hearts
It takes an abandoned child within a wounded woman
That little girl who fears
The one who birthed love into her
May leave
The smell and taste of nothingness will always linger
At each and every possibility
No sister. This is deeper than a fear or broken
conditioning
To rebuild the same events
To relive the same moments...
Secretly hoping this time, time will stay
This time my time may remain...
The time you yearn will come in time
Your heart and mind unite
The choice of consciousness
Because time is consistently changing...
Change according to your Choices!
Not your E-Motion-Less...

Officially Crazy

Officially crazy
Read these lyrics oh baby
Diagnosed: mentally unstable.
Didn't you know?
I wear it so well though...
What's it called??
That Bi-bi polarity shit!
Damn my Mister love me so good
Be bruising me to mark his territory
Using me whilst undermining me
Blaming the tears I cry on my twisted mind
That's right; he's right!!!
As of right now
I am officially CRAZY
Motherfucker didn't know
What a real crazy look like...
Haha
Imma show him alright!??
Put some fear, tame my Mister
Show him who the fuck Karma is!
Imma just give you a preview of what's about to go down
As soon as this restrain jacket comes down:

I am crazy for loving you
I was crazy for giving you everything I had
And now I am left even more crazy
Cause you didn't give me the same love back;
You took my mind, my name my money
Even the air I breathe
You have so much fun with it
Hence why you refuse to leave
But I too refuse to lay my life down for you
Especially with you being on this quest
Or is it a test!?
I wonder how you'd feel
If you managed to kill me!?
Probably just another crazy woman
Lying naked lifeless
Go on and blame me
The moons shifts & moods swings
Even though it was you who made me
If there's anything you gave me
Oh baby
It was this crazy

Why should I strive to keep an art, which is despised by its own canvas??!
How can I paint the picture when a deserted throne is reflected by my own reflection?
I lay awakened, hurt and unprotected
I roar for you
You hunt for me...
I roar for you
Whilst you make prey of me...

Raw Lotion on our Ships

Say you're tired of my attitude?
We both know after Eye there's no substitute
Since when does the Truth sounds like me nagging?
Or maybe am just a tiny broken like ya
Maybe me too am so frustrated feeling so lonely right next to you
World War 3 and my Lover is my enemy
Oh, male Reflection
To understand who I am, you must overcome who you are
You are king to my kingdom
Yet you keep choosing a system of Slavery over me
A God of the laws, why must you live like a fugitive?
A lion of all wilderness
How can you insist on living under water like a fish???
I know your back still hurts
From the cuts on our ancestors broken stolen souls
Our blood remains abundant
Splashed, Spilled, Spread
Who knows Sacrificed maybe...
But I am just your nagging black woman
What do I know?
As if it isn't her who tends to the wounds which burn you today
As if it isn't her who needs you so desperately for her protection
And the protection of your cubs

As if it is not her trauma too
Having laid with the master who marked you
Like a beast, Praise Caesar, what else could I do...?
Oh Brother, stolen broken reflection
A king to my kingdom
Let your bondage not turn you away from your responsibility
Which is me, our kids and our village
Let not those chains make you forget your throne
No diamond nor precious metal shines brighter than you
Not a whole eternal slavery can accomplish diminishing the lights of you
A true Son of the Sun Hue are
An unknowing God conditioned on reverse
To hate yourselves becoming whom you hate so
There's a psychology of the pains inflicted transmitted through DNA
Eye need you more than you need yourself
What is your freedom?
When mother nature was being raped
It was us who served them
When every kind was claiming land
We weren't allowed to
So now I am a beast for seeking Normality
Now we're not fit for society
You despise your melanated skin
Relax the roots of your crown in hopes you'll be accepted by

The system who did this to you
It's 2018, my wisdom is your strength, your strength
is my wisdom
We can break these chains today
We must embrace true freedom as I say
Is the government of back then, not the same as we
know now!?

Let me calm your desperation
Can you hear the drums in your heart?
Listen to your children's laughter a while
Do you remember your own?
Or instead you snap uncomfortably because it's gotten
so difficult
To feel your own soul!!!?
Oh brother, lover
Without you I cannot be whole
It is you who teaches our offspring to be mighty
and strong
Only you can love me and make this battle for
justice all worth
You may not have it all – because having is an illusion
And that's why I nag because...
My king, we need no Thing
We are it ALL

Oh Brother, stolen broken reflection
A king to my kingdom

Let your bondage not turn you away from your
responsibility
Which is me, our kids and our village
Let not those chains make you forget your throne
No diamond nor precious metal shines
brighter than you
Not a whole eternal slavery can accomplish diminishing
the lights of you
A true Son of the Sun Hue are
An unknowing God conditioned on reverse
To hate yourselves becoming whom you hate so
There's a psychology of the pains inflicted transmitted
through DNA
No diamond nor precious metal shines
brighter than you
Not a whole eternal slavery can accomplish diminishing
the lights of you
A true Son of the Sun Hue are

Dear Brother

Oh brother
I know You are angry
I am angry too
I am already fighting myself
I cannot fight you
Oh lover
Pleasurer, demander
Breath taker
Life giver
Oh husband
take not the seed
Off the ground and throw it
It needs time, it takes patience
Oh father
Provider, educator
Creator, Haven
Protector
Shelter to my magic
Oh son
Son of my womb
Universe of my vows
Take heed
And follow your own heart's
Footsteps
I will always be your Goddess
Regardless of who you are to me

I will always love you
Yet put me first
As I have always taught you to do.

Silent Leader

Woman
Remain Strong
You are the healers
Makers of this world
Serve your husband your partner
Gather and guard his gold
For its shine depends on your heart
Feed his mind, his body, his soul
You are not his trophy
You are his master
Quietly giving more and more
So what, you're sore? You're sore!
He appreciates you for you
Not the seeds you bore
When you find your worth
When you learn your whole
You will realise, he is everything you're here for!
His growth lies in your work

Love him and you will love yourself...

Sleep with an eye open to watch over his head.
Prepare him for the war ahead
Be his strength instead of the reason he fails

Woman
You are King
You are lion
Endlessly kind
Firm like iron
Understand your place
This is my siren

Rise up woman
The war has started

Polarity of Love

Do you still remember the first time you saw my wings?
Amongst all that maya surrounded by all those jins?
I saw you and all you could see was me!?
In hate I loved you. Whilst in pain you loved me.
How could we have built such a divine sanctuary?
Your presence triggers my animalistic instincts
You are the element of opportunity
To fulfil my natural sinful desires...
The way you rub your beard on my neck
Leaving your scent lingering through my skin
Your gaze shoots electricity harmoniously through my spine...
Leaving my body shivering in ecstasy
By a basic thought of the things we do...
Your scent inspires me to write endless tales of truth
My body is paper to your pen,
Oh God,
Write in me the secrets that are relevant...
I am melted butter in the mighty hands of your consciousness...
Lost in the rivers of my flow with your current...
Our current situation is constant

Female Expressions

The body of a woman
Regardless of its shape or shade
Independently of its size or age
A contemplation of gracious art
Her womb brings the warmth
Her incubator promotes growth
She is as fertile as fertility itself
Having mastered the ability
To 7 times fold anything you propose
Yet I'd suppose you'd listen
Still you won't...
She constantly feels mother's nature neglect
Upon herself...
Because you're willing to sacrifice
everything that sustains your life
to feed an ego that's temporary
Now tell me,
If you comprehend the purpose of this piece!
Are you willing to work towards world peace?
She'll forever love you
And I'll just leave you with this

*When loving them
is more about loving you.*

The Birthing

Having broken down for days which turned into nights
Weeks which so quickly multiplied into months
Every single year went by so slowly
Each moment an eternity
Little did I know it was just my destiny
All my dreams in my lap all at once
I just didn't know what to do with it!!!
I just didn't recognise their seeds,
Neither did I have a clue how to plant dreams...
Who said crying's main use was expressing pain?
Didn't you know contracting pains are found to be releasing!?
Enabling the opening of a cervix to birth a new life...
The tears you cry, when you finally just make it
To the other side...
Enabling the healing of the self, birthing a purer Cell
Whatever it takes
A lonely soul, unafraid
Searching things, places and others as lovers
When what she seeks is Herself...
Even God in 'person' couldn't satisfy

A Better Love

Deserted by the man who drove her to insanity
Abandoned in the desert of her emotions...
In the wilderness of her anguish
She needed that which she casted away
After the explosion
Came the silence
Is it serenity? Or death?
Why am I surprised, indulged in such a delicacy?
Of course my plate is empty now.
Yet my soul is full, so filled
Why then am I fooled, tricked...
By a simple empty plate...?
Now that I come to think about it;
Loving another was never external...
All the love stories, affairs and connections
Were truly all about finding me...
How I eluded myself with an external lover
Whilst seducing myself into the waves of Self-Love
What I loved about all the men and women I've lusted for
It was the reflection of my own ability of loving me...

Now that it's clear to see,
Now that I can safely be honest within
Seen as the truth is all there is
Sitting here watching the world like a show
We're constantly creating hells surrounding us...
Then we cry, desperately not
understanding it was all us...
Just let your soul burn in your created hell
Until it purifies...
Qualifying it for truth
Only then will you know you...
Only then you know how much you love you...

Eye Am's

True Love is having it, not wanting it
To love me you have got to love me as love is
Not want me as you desire me to fulfil
you & your agenda
I am
I just am.... who Eye am!
Eye am does not include your expectations
Eye am does not incorporate me as your possession
Even if I am as I am desperately in love with you...
Eye am doesn't come in as a contract
And cannot be influenced unless it chooses to be
influenced so
Eye am follows only the laws of nature
Which are her own laws
Eye am wants nothing
Loves All & everything of the ALL
Eye am knows herself now
Loves her essence in every season
If not, then she must continue her quest
Until she finds hers, Eye am

Her

She was a flame sparked in hell when heaven was a pile of wood...
The Master glared at her in fear...
The silent wind wasn't enough to block his soul which torrentially screamed...
Who is this?
Where did it come from?
Her fierce
A desperate hunger and thirst in her eye...
Familiar yet unrecognisable
She's unafraid of anything and everything...
She's immune to the pains and aches now...
The forces of nature seek revenge for each of her spilled blood...
Each of her fallen tears...
Her only craft is gratitude and forgiveness...
Unaware of her royal soul
All these army guides orbiting around her...
Knows not hers I am
So evident, so far away
Yet flowing gracefully to where her kind belongs...
I am who I am
So more, no less

As above so below
A flame sparked in Hell
When heaven was just a pile of wood...

Part 2

360 Shades of Soul

360 Degrees of the Love Cycle

Spring Love
Summer Love
Autumn Love
Winter Love

Are you aware of your Seasons?

Moistured Scriptures

(Spring)

As she listens to his wisdom speech
Through lust so cunningly her love flame creeps
Secretly yearning to be the scripture on his lips
The parables his consciousness seeks
The one he fears most
For the awareness of being his upmost beloved
A regular broken illusion
Revealed by the prophet professor
Whom eagerly pleased to bow
Surrendering to her pleasure
In the luxurious dusty grounds of nature
Perpetrated in such Godly leisure
Spread legs wide like demon wings
Finally sailing through darkness
Pulled by the current of her fluids
Each corner of her river wilderness explored
Oh, what is this wilderness he wonders
Impotent to the magic of her body
Conscious at-traction
Able to drive a God to his knees
Exchanging thy celibacy
For a moment of such sin
By whom knows its illusions yet commits...
May eye be the snake in your tree
The scriptures deeper than your lips can bring
Embrace me like the Sanskrit of thy soul peak

Drink of my fountain as your aura makes her drip...
Cleanse you in my waters,
Electrified by your presence...
Use me, find in me all the love you yearn to
give our world
Beloved of my heart
Betrothed due to our crime
Because Soul paths prove entwined
Beyond the mind's ability to understand
So, you & Eye create
Eye the scriptures
You the preacher of her love!
Taste me before you love them
Flavour my passion as you immerse in
Universal Rhythms
Dance to the beat of my heart as you lead
Eye submits
Bowing and rocking to each bang of your drum...
She the scriptures,
He the preacher lips

Untitled 2

(Autumn)

When I finally found a man of God's calibre
He gave me a piece of my own medicine...
And I... loved every drop of it...
Soul pleasure
Moments, sensations to treasure
Invisible, tangible portals
Surrounding all around us
Sweet taste all over my tongue
Loving lusting together as one
The hand which did not rub my body,
Penetrated this ecstasy into me...
To be continued...

God's Love

(Summer)

I much rather make your eternity
My God, Oh God
Reflection you are of Eye
What a natural ecstasy
Bind me in truth
Tie me in your nature
Which is also mine
Holding my hair firmly in your warrior's fist
Your power delivers safety in my kingdom
But your wisdom is Everything
Kill me and bring me back to life
Baptise me in your wisdom
Sacred is thy semen
My womb a portal to the sea men into our realm
My flowing rivers are the only confirmation needed
That it's not pain but pleasure
Oh Alchemist
Merging your magnetic field into mine
Your scent is home...
Wasting no elements
We become our original One
$1 + 1 = 3 = 0 = circle = 99 = 96 = 69 = 66$
What a perfect flow
Our secret solar system of love
Holy water drops from my eyes
Anointing each and all of his chakras

I cannot believe I found you in this life time...
Choke me with your love until I pass out!
Then meet me in my dreams and love me again
Oh Mathematician
Work me out
Find my X, my G all my letters
Add me, divide you, estimate US
We already know the formula it is you in me
Just don't stop penetrating my mind
Gazing right into the tunnel of my Eye
Hold on to my thighs as you hold on to your burning Soul
Scientist of my heart
My healer, you alone break down these walls
Eradicating this solitude of mine with each kiss
Reflection of my dreams
Your genuine love does not go amiss...
I surrender to your anaconda
I belong to the rules of your kingdom
Gladly accept, enjoy each punishment
Which belongs to me
Losing control, my king pulls me back to the path
Like a child distracted by a butterfly
'Proceed with caution my Queen'
I bow to my king, and he bows to me – his Goddess
My juices is all he desires
Only a God can replenish the Soul
In such intense manner
Don't take your skin off of mine

Keep your Soul inside me
In his chamber of peace, I found my throne
Reptilian, lover of this dome...
So glad I am Thy wife...
Betrothed yet detached

Reptilian

(Summer)

You and I can stop the time
Baby, our love numbs death
How the density of the air changes when you're around
When I am around you
How you arouse my chakras
A magnet to you my iron
A river to your waters
He said he'd blow a healing cloud into my cervix
He penetrates me without laying a finger on my skin
Breathes with me
Steals my breath
Replacing it with pleasure
We fly into each other's realms
Dimensions together, through portals and passages
We exist also in so many other worlds
And physical appearances...
He's my human, my male
My God and saviour, my Devil oppressor
He's my alien reptilian
He's the one and only able
Meant to keep my Soul on fire
The one I love
The spark to my flame
Whom I belong to
My lion

Immortal Love

(Autumn)

If tasting, indulging in your love
If materialising the love of God
Makes you mortal...
Reflection perfection
Walk away in your matter
You're forever entwined
with my flame in Spirit anyway...

I much rather make your eternity
I much rather fulfil your ascension
Deserted yet chosen
Abandoned, though ever loved

If holding me in your safety
If materialising the essence of this Goddess
Makes me mortal!!?
Reflection perfection
Oh Alchemist – walk away with all your gold
I'll be forever infused
Into the flame of your Soul
I much rather love you in silence
Feel you in stillness
Be the love you love
Rather than who
You lay
&
Become mortal with...

Marinated

(Summer)

Marinated in warm water
Like my emotions immersed in your milky love...
My consciousness travelling through pleasurable lands
with yours
This euphoric electricity that intensifies
as it rushes through the insides of my ligaments...
Make your way into me as only you know how...
Come into Eye until you see you through my eyes
Observe how your eyes gaze back ever so bright,
Each and every time
Your gaze line crosses mine...
Come into me until you learn to love yourself how
Eye love you...
Let's re-write Adonis & Venus of 2018

A writer without a lover is but a dreamer without
imagination...

Underneath

(Autumn)

I take off my red & black lingerie...
Untouched, ready
Yet again deserted
By her own expectations
Disappointed
Naked all in her one
Without her One
Is it done?
If he's won...
Just hasn't left
Leaving me wondering am I dead yet!?
Deserted yes
Still disturbed
By the sudden abandonment
Of such lingering lover
Pierced deep in my heart
Antagonising
Patronising my right to happiness
Why does he hurt if he's not here...?
Was freedom not what Eye needed...?
Naked,
No red nor black silk upon my skin...

Jealous God

(Winter)

If my God is a jealous One
How can I submit me without jealousy!??
How do I release these fears??
How do I trust he'll spank them out through
pleasurable pain!?
If thy rod is not mine alone
Please answer my Eye beloved:
Why are they in between our All One!??
When will you open the floodgates to thy truth!?
Lies, illusions, traps aren't bait for Goddesses...
What kind of love or loneliness
Must cause me to fall for such a false trap...?
What kind of test of nature
To cause her heart to yearn loneliness
Over my God's warmth over another her
What must I learn with this throbbing ache??
When jealousy is embedded in his very sense.
The scent of her fake hair
Which compares not to the Goddess natural Cell...
The scratches of her acrylic nails on your wings
Whom could never come close
Were they as real as mine...?
Leaving me in jealousy, you fly to her...
Hear her smiles which belong to my heart...!
How can you submit to lies, who's truth is so visible...?

Poker Face

(Winter)

Turn the other cheek;
Shall it mean continue hurting me?
Is the nature of a queen, to live as slave of her king?
Is my throne a dungeon where I live...?
Beside my glorious, mighty king
Invisible – I am to his eye.
Concubines scent rubbed on his chest;
Who am I? I ask
So often, quietly, inside...
Thrown tears tear their own tides...
Likewise, I struggle loving my lover oppressor.
King of kings, lord of Lords
Entwined with whom he claims to be a nobody!
His one and only beloved, chosen...
Who am I??
Guess I should have asked, had Eye been asked...
An army ready to set off to war for my heart,
Eager for the ideals of love.
As kings lock up alchemists for gold – yet
appreciates it Not!
Which cheek must I turn?
If not the other?
Rather my whole Eye to me!?!
Before a mind was written, it had been thought of...
No, my king, for the love of your kingdom
You shouldn't provoke my other cheek,
Is mother nature's other cheek not a karma's swing?

Poisoned Antidote

(Winter)

Oh God, my God beloved
I no longer love you in this flesh
No longer yearn the touch
The hurricane tsunami you spark in my chest
You're such a fire
Which blinds me to my own lava
Stolen of who I am
Flesh embodies the irresistible liar
Dispersing my senses
Contradicting the focus, he leads
Blinded in nothingness she seeks
Exactly how Eye too enjoy each sip
His wine so fine which drunken me not
Rather awakened such he knew not existent
Now naked, awakened awaiting
Observant of her gaze all over your magnetic field
No!
I choose not belong to this In-sanity
Yes!
Let her have you the way you once wanted me
May she pave the Karma
Fleshly Gods aren't excused
Conduct your purpose purposefully
How could he a student
Presented as Master & teacher
Crafted such witch??

Loneliness is the cause of such bliss
Temporary illusion
She drank her own potion
For the ecstasy his antidote does not bring
How can the love of God be the poison??
To bring her to her knees
Eye love him
I love him not...

Obsession Lover

(Spring, April showers)

Obsession takes over consciousness
Desires enhancing loving lusted moments
Self-Neglect creates ideologies of what one seeks within
Reflected through a broken wish upon a man...
Still... ever so still the emptiness
Eager, so eager to fulfil
A secret yearn
Such happiness does not exist
A deep desire
Tongues alone do not bring
Words don't decipher blooms
Although entwine you in its blues
All of a sudden, all she's strived for dissipates away
Like her inner child's wish upon a star
No day to come other than today
No better tomorrow than what she'd created
A Goddess
A Sexual
A Celibate

To My Dear Beloved,

(Spring)

A perfect Reflection, Brother, lover friend.
Desired betrothed yet liberated through detachment...
Enhanced through unconditional love
Yet denied by each conditionality of such worldly love...
If your heart causes your Goddess to fall – indeed pluck it out...
If her heart demands such needs of comfort your arms cannot reach
May Eye find the Universe's lone... Alone as ALL ONE
Beloved, so beloved
Never have I encountered another as such...
You are far more, yet further less
So perfect, perfection does not compare...
Through Eye thy cosmos send a message...
For you help me on my Soul Journey
Grateful & Great – filled Eye became further more...
far less...
Tell me if your heart beats inner her Stand...?
The gift you gave me was of LOVE
The Initiation you planted in her was of your touch
A hold the Atlantic couldn't prevent
Neither of US protect
Do not fine her ownership!
For Gods do not belong – neither do they own...
Do Not fine the other sisters, my sister Goddesses
For each were born infused in that which they belong...

You gave me nothing which Eye did not give to you!!!
You taught me nothing which Eye did not
taught You too!!
Reflection Perfection beware for I love YOU
A Goddess' love is such of a sharp sword
Cuts all and cries alone whilst her beloveds
bleed unsure...
Reflection Perfection beware for I love EYE
Eye's love needs nothing, less is so much more...
Curls and cries, exhaling the excruciating salt out of
each tear...
Give no fear, keep it or rather allow me releasing it...
A prophet, messiah
Learns that which he teaches
Keeps that which he preaches
Eye feel you – far more than Eye tell you
Eye feel those other Goddesses...
I thought you knew who I AM
But you confused God's idea of Her own GOD...
You don't know the energies you pick up
Do not deliver this to another
Cleansing, clearing is essential
My training course goes beyond things I'm prepared to
share with you...
Don't give my lessons to another...
As you share your juices entwined with them...
Perhaps this letter is more for Eye than it is for you
To decrease this clinginess to live

To erode this desire to share, reflect my beauty
with you...
Despite it all
Eye come from Truth
Truth is where Eye go
& in truth each and everyone
Is Born
Reborn
With US or without US
As we know it
As we flow it
Reflection Perfection
Eye am grateful to have encountered your God
Eye am grateful I was worthy to learn thy Lucipher
With love, light, darkness
& all the colours in between

Ugly Truth

(Summer)

Words don't move my heart
No! Not anymore.
Money doesn't guarantee safety
No! We can't buy what doesn't exist
Poetry releases, reveals
Those things...
Dramas sprouting from hidden feelings
Covered, suppressed such inadequate fears
That's all there is within the pretty
Ahhh – that ugly hard truth
Within that beautiful you seek – you find the truth of its opposite.
True beauty is the liberation of knowing how ugly you really are
Yet still so lovable
As we face the toughest battles of our lives
Most die, leaving nothing but a mask behind
Pass it on to their offspring
With the pressure and promise of inadequacy
Till the end of time – never quite knowing why

No! not anymore!
Not with Eye
Let us rise in our truth and our darkness
Little did we know: wearing our ugly is the most
Beautiful Universal truth!
Eye invite you to be yourself
Today, tonight, tomorrow and forever
Your ugly is so beautiful

Love Hack

(*Autumn*)

I have a message within me
That is beyond me
Even wonder how have I been carrying this!?
So fearful to release
In speech
On sound
Heart palpitates
Cannot keep still
How do I spill!!??
The anxiety of the love hack...?
How can we teach ourselves love?
When we were unloved!??
How do I give birth, when I was un-birthed!?
Why do I search for love, when my lover makers didn't yearn to love me!??
Self... Cell
Peace of being
What is love but a word describing it!?
The masses seeking it,
Even make believe they are buying it...

What is love?
If it brings not peace of being?
Who shall seek love??
If not those who lack in it?
What can love be to me???
Within our peace of living?
But another branding word, set up to sell to me!!
Who can I be if I know not peace?
Just another fool with a branded package,
With love and a barcode stamped on it.

Kiss Her

(Summer)

Kiss her deeper
Entice each hump of her heart
Ride it with passion
As a God tames His mind
Until it melts
Like the wetness of her love...
Not her wrath
Never must you spark her wrath
If you just learn how to kiss her deeper...
Beyond the wetness;
Beyond the thickening of her fluids!
Kiss her deeper
Kiss her shame and secrets
Embrace all corners,
Especially where it seems unreachable...
Savour her love in ways not yet existent!
Kiss her deeper in each and every day of your life
Kiss her with your lips
Kiss her with each gaze each time you look at her
Kiss her deeper
Because she can't wait to kiss you back

A God After a Woman's Heart

(Summer)

He was a God after my own heart
Unconditional love having
Kingdom having
Hell and Heaven having
But Eye.. I was so human in His hands...
This Goddess was so vulnerable in His heavenly chambers...
So weak through each of His devilish desires...
Eye am just an apple which brings God's to their knees...
Temptation deemed as sin
At the centre of Eye stands tree.
Eye am the wisdom snake loving God's lust so innocently.
He is the God after my own heart!
So God
So Supreme
Eye ever so humble yet glorified through thee
The secret gardens of truth...
Limiting sensations of rules
Entwined in an existence of me and you.
What else is a God supposed to do?
But love thyself as a creator loves his creation!?!?
Unleash love where love is needed
Write tales filled with metaphors,
Marinated with the essence of all things
Yet exclusive for only those truly able to savour it.

Eye am the snake, Womb-Mother
Eye whom holds the womb
Portal of living knowledge
At the centre of Me
The wisdom apple is found within
You

Ankhed

(Summer)

When his lips speak
My inner ligaments spring
As his gaze lingers
Electric sparks stroll through my skin...
His Mighty words of wisdom

Admires my most divine nature
How deep such lover goes
Exploring places where Nothing & ALL belongs
How fervent is the lover of her Mind
Seduced, in trance & sight of his might...
"More & more" silently she cries
With fire burning through her eyes...
Touches Eye so deep, such sweet flavors
Rubbed on my Soul peak
Without laying a finger...
How intense his Might lingers
Loving lusting,
Her body trembles to pleasures so explicit...
Restless, like ecstasy pumping through her arteries...
God am Eye speechless...??

Make her feel without your fingers;
Hear her scream for your physical...
As you deepen on her with your psychic abilities
Enjoy her mind as a child upon a playground...
Release your might,
Upon her heart
Such God makes art upon a Goddess' throne & dome...
Abstract emotions ever flowing to the blossom
of her Love

Goddess Magic

(Spring)

Take time to breathe
Gently, mindfully, carefully
As you apply your eyeliner...
Smudge your soul with sage to cleanse,
As you wipe out the corners of your lips removing extra lipstick.
Look into the mirror of your soul
Breathe in and out peacefully
Blending the blusher evenly...
Follow your own breath
Till it guides you to your own centre...
Discover how to connect with nature
Practice intuition by focusing all of your mental.
Take your soul through the process of ascension
Then when you gaze at him,
Through the dim moon light
Squeeze your root chakra
Pulling onto his 3rd eye with yours like a magnet.
Engage your sacral chakra
Swerve them in alignment with his heartbeat.
Allow his nature to strip you off your fears
Merge into his energy like a mermaid in the ocean
Loving him unconditionally
Each drop, each wave, each grain of salt...
Home sweet home
This embrace is equivalent to an ocean of love

That strong humble face awaiting her caress
Reveal your chakras as you dance for him
Unleash your fluorescent colours
Healing him down as you heal yourself up
Red
Orange
Yellow
Green
Blue
Indigo
Purple
There is power in all that you do
Intentionally or via external influence and stimuli.
Every action is a manifestation ritual
So, go and manifest your dreams
Your magic is in the palms of your hands
You are magical

Love Me Like the Sun

(Autumn)

Love me how Earth loves the Sun,
Orbit around me like your existence depends on it...
So naturally,
Responding to the pulls of my Solar Inner energy...
Love me how planet Earth loves the Sun!
Search for me how winter yearns its warmth,
Indulge in each ray of me as one does through winter solstice...
Love me just how Earth loves the Sun,
Not too close or you'd get burnt, three steps back to be exact!!
May I feed you my light & out of your world my love extract...
Love me like the Sun,
A planet, a world like you
Is all that keeps these flames burning...
To see you rotate, as you gaze with your Soul onto me...
Eye am here – day & night
So love me like the Sun
When you see it & when you don't
Not too far, not too close...
Like the Sun Beloved...
May the Sun guide you home
Into unconditional love

About the Author

Indi Writes, natural healer, meditation guru and coach is on a quest to provide individuals with the courage and compassion they need, to heal and transform their lives through poetry. Indi runs her spiritual healing business *Womanhood2Goddesshood* and through exclusive spiritual coaching and meditation, assists individuals in finding and identifying with what their soul truly seeks.

www.ingramcontent.com/pod-product-compliance
Lightning Source LLC
Chambersburg PA
CBHW070952080526
44587CB00015B/2282